GEORGES BRAQUE

JACQUES DAMASE

Georges Braque

BLANDFORD PRESS
LONDON

editor: Anthony Bosman

translation: Tony White

lay-out: Wim van Stek and Aart Verhoeven

photography: Daniel Frasnay, Paris

First published in the English edition in 1963

by Blandford Press Ltd. London

reproduction rights 1963: A.D.A.G.P., Paris

© 1963: and printed in Holland by The Ysel Press Ltd. Deventer

GEORGES BRAQUE

Braque, whose name is one of the most celebrated in painting, has remained essentially a calm, quiet man, who does not often let himself be photographed, who is not often seen in public, and who, even at the age of eighty, tries every day to perfect his work, always adding something new, something better.

He is seldom seen in society—in fact, he has never been seen in it. He entertains his friends well, and lives either in his house near the Parc Montsouris in Paris, or in his beautiful Normandy village of Varengeville, which stands on a cliff, near the sea.

The painter's life makes a fine story, an almost exemplary one. The Father of Cubism (with Picasso), he has since 1907 played a leading part in the history of painting.

He was born on May 13, 1882, in Argenteuil, near Paris. His father owned a house-painting firm, and was himself an amateur artist. Eight years after Georges was born, his family settled in Le Havre; hence the common notion that Braque is from Normandy. He studied at the local École des Beaux-Arts, learned to play the flute with the brother of Raoul Dufy (whom he knew also), returned to his father as an apprentice, and then went to Paris to work for a decorating firm. This was where he learned the technique of imitation wood and imitation marble (which is now much used), and also his skill in reproducing and drawing letters and characters, which he later exploited in various pictures.

From 1900 onwards, then, he lived in Paris and, for two years, frequented art schools, studios, and academies. Finally, in 1906, he exhibited six canvases at the Salon des Indépendants, spent the summer in Antwerp with the painter Othon Friesz (whom he had known at Le Havre) and the autumn in the Midi—at L'Estaque, near Marseilles—where he began to paint in the Fauve manner, thanks to his friend Friesz, who introduced him to the new trend.

The Fauvism that Braque practised, after a mild flirtation with impressionism, came in reaction against the latter: a violent reaction against the disappearance of space and in favour of an atmospheric use of light; against its meticulous and often arbitrary analysis; and finally, and most important, against a technical facility which had supplanted a proven aesthetic: "open-air" painting. What mattered to the Fauves, as one critic said, was colour not in its actual truth, but in its component value. For them a picture was a composition, not a reproduction; a plastic sequence, not an anecdotal tableau; an organization of coloured stresses.

From this point on, Braque's immense personality began to emerge. For, while he became a Fauve through the influence of Friesz, Dufy, and others, he was never so extreme as most of the Fauves.

The Revelation of Cézanne: the Cylinder, the Sphere, the Cone

Braque returned to Paris but did not like it there. He again left for the South and settled once more at L'Estaque, in search of the kind of light he needed to inspire him. The pictures which he made of the countryside and the hills, the port, and the wharves were all Fauve, with plenty of colour and, above all, a solid construction. These paintings sold very quickly. In fact, in October, 1905, the art dealer Daniel Henri Kahnweiler opened his famous gallery at 28 Rue Vignon; he already owned pictures by Derain, Picasso, Vlaminck, and Van Dongen. He

soon bought his first picture from Braque and, shortly after-wards, his entire output.

Braque went to La Ciotat again with Friesz, and painted the wonderful pink landscape (p. 21); but in the autumn Cézanne's influence began to make itself felt: the colours lost their bright-ness, and browns and greys became dominant.

From Cézanne Braque learned the discipline of architecture. In the autumn of 1907, an important retrospective exhibition of the Aix master [Cézanne], who had just died, opened in Paris and on this occasion one of his letters to Émile Bernard was published: "Allow me to repeat what I told you here: to deal with nature by means of the cylinder, the sphere, and the cone all placed in perspective . . . and the lines parallel to the horizon give breadth, as if by a reaction of nature. The lines perpendicular to this horizon give depth. Because nature, for us men, exists more in depth than on the surface . . ."

There it was, in that letter: the method—the recipe, if you like—for using cubism; and artists, particularly Braque, were not long in putting it into practice.

7

Photograph of the artist

It was at this time that Kahnweiler also introduced him to Picasso, who was living at the Bateau-Lavoir in Montmartre, surrounded by numerous friends: Gertrude and Leo Stein, Apollinaire, Max Jacob, Juan Gris, and others. This is how an eye-witness reported it: Picasso was then working on his *"Demoiselles d'Avignon"* (the name was inspired by the *demoiselles* of easy virtue who worked in the Rue d'Avignon); the reflective, methodical Braque gazed at the canvas, riveted to the spot with astonishment: "Look," he said to Picasso, "I don't care what you say, but you paint as if you wanted to make us eat tow or drink petrol, in order to spit fire!"

Picasso's *"Demoiselles d'Avignon"*, however, had not yet come under the influence of cubism or of Cézanne; it stands between the famous *camaïeux* of his Blue Period, and the influence of Negro masks; about the latter, though, some critics disagree, insisting that it was not Negro art, as is thought, which influenced Picasso, but primitive Catalan art.

In any case, the shock of Picasso's painting may have made Braque even more anxious to change his style. He did a nude (p. 22) influenced by the *"Demoiselles"*, which is apparently the only work of Picasso's that influenced him. But it still was not cubism.

The Arrival of Cubism

It was in 1907-8, in front of a picture by Braque, called "Houses at L'Estaque"(p. 23), that the word "cubes" was first mentioned. Several people claim to have originated it, while others maintain that it was Matisse who, looking at this picture, said: "You'd think they were little cubes." Eventually, in 1909, discussing another landscape and a still life by Braque, Louis Vauxelles referred in *Gil Blas* to "these strange cubic oddities" and the term "cubism" was launched.

9

This new style of painting was in the air: others were anticipating it, but Braque was the first to practise it, and the only one besides Picasso to practise it authoritatively. It was the beginning of a wonderful adventure for the two. "From 1909 on," says Braque, "Picasso and I have worked in perfect harmony, in the same state of mind, and it is obvious that if we had not met, all this would never have happened. But it had to be this way."

In 1907-9, pre-cubism, beginning with Cézanne, had made use of geometrical components, but Braque was striving to fill space, leaving no gaps, and to further this unity, he limited his palette to a few colours, particularly ochres and greens, in an almost *camaieux* effect.

Cubism, from 1910 to 1914, no longer used the cube itself, but aimed at "a geometric simultaneity in the representation of objects."

In 1910 came analytic cubism. "As soon as I became convinced that it was necessary to get rid of the model," Braque goes on to say, "it was not so very easy ... But I was set on it, and the separation was made by means of instinctive efforts ... At such moments one obeys an almost unconscious imperative. One does not know just what will come of it. It is an adventure; the conscious mind plays no part in it."

"What attracted me especially," he once confided to Dora Vallier—and it was the guiding principle of cubism—"was the new materialization of space which I perceived."

In 1911 the cubist works of Braque became less immediately intelligible. The elements of form appear upon first examination, but the form itself is only with difficulty reconstituted by the eye. He continued his work in close collaboration with Picasso and stayed with him in Céret and in Sorgues (pp. 24, 25).

"Picasso and I said things to each other during those years there that no one will ever say again, that no one would know how

10

to say, that no one would be able to comprehend—things that could not be comprehended—things which have given us so much joy and which will end with us . . ."

In 1912 Braque began to use paper pasted to the canvas, creating contrasting planes. Then there were letters, characters, which he was the first to introduce into a painting. He soon went so far as to use sand. Then when his collages (paper pasted onto canvas) no longer satisfied him, he preferred something that would be more complicated and so he deceived the eye with false paper, false wood, false marble, using the technique of the decorative painter that he had learned from his father (p. 26). Between the years 1910 and 1914, though, as we know, he returned to the Midi, he soon abandoned landscapes and portraits and restricted himself to still lifes, sometimes in ovoid form.

By introducing paper stuck on canvas, letters, and sand, Braque created a new technique. He has continued to make use of it until today, "whenever he feels the need to create some spectacular poetic effect."

During this entire period, it is sometimes difficult to distinguish Braque's paintings from Picasso's; yet each time I compare them, I find that Braque's are more beautiful, more complete, more like paintings, whereas Picasso's remain more like the work of a draftsman.

When war was declared, Braque was called up as a sergeant, conducted himself admirably at the front, and was so seriously wounded in the head that a trepanation was necessary. Discharged in 1917, he took many months to recover.

Was this the end of cubism? Not at all. Meanwhile, Picasso, a Spaniard and therefore not subject to conscription, went on with his experiments. Braque also, after a long convalescence, set to work again; but, while still picking up the threads where he left off, he made a new departure with another conception. He now began to use a synthetic cubism: the object seen in all its real and imagined possibilities; depth was no longer a matter of *trompe-l'oeil,* but a mere suggestion. The space of Renaissance art was abolished. Each component of the object (real or imaginary) had to be seen from a particular angle, chosen and constructed so that it entered into the organized rhythm of the picture. Space became the juxtaposition of images on planes. Light was sparsely indicated in the various components; although its colour did not vary much, it was inherent and had to be incorporated into the object, though without defining it or constructing it. Because of these planes with facets, the drawing became intense. Later it was to become anonymous, because every painter submitted to it, without trying to assert his individuality, and all cubist painters freely used the same common themes: still lifes, compositions with violins or mandolins, jugs, pedestal tables . . . But in his choice of colours, Braque was, as during his Fauve period, the subtlest: a nacreous profusion of pale and ivory tones.

Construction through Colour

Braque's art, from 1918 until 1934, seems to have veered towards the classical. His predilection for still lifes and interiors (p. 27), the slow and deep reflection which always lay beneath his plastic creations, the nobility of his compositions, and the sober gravity of his palette made him one of the great masters of French art.

In the early days of cubism, Braque used to say: "I like the rule that corrects emotion." But sometimes emotion corrects the rule, and this is what must have happened about 1918-20, after the cubist period. He still had to find his own solution.

From 1920 on, he strove after the most classical of ideals: combining sculptural representations with architectural bases.

From 1922 to 1925, he was a neo-classicist: his basket bearers and his women carrying fruit (p. 28) are typical examples.

In 1927, he once again introduced bright tones and rediscovered his taste for colour.

The year 1929 saw a new vitality of line and colour. Arabesques increased during the course of the next few years. Braque was also inspired by Greek mythology and the designs of Hellenic vases to return to figures, but, in general, he was most concerned with composition and with bold combinations. Picasso's logic is completely intuitive; Braque's is more deductive. Braque observes and then creates; Picasso, on the contrary, transforms Cézanne-like intentions—he does not observe nature, he thinks it.

The painter has expressed himself admirably on this subject:

"We reintegrated colour with paper stuck on canvas. What we were trying to do has not always been very well understood, yet it is very simple. We wanted to make colour independent of form, give it autonomy. I think the critics were very shocked by the materials used, which they did not find sufficiently 'noble'. We thought, on the contrary, that they were of great poetic interest."

His discovery of Cézanne helped him, as we have seen, to master his palette and, throughout the entire cubist period, he stuck to blue, ochre, and green monochromes, to whites and blacks highlighted with light browns, to the artificial wood which obsessed the entire generation, and to those sad 1914 wallpaper colours which everyone worked into his paintings in one way or another.

Towards 1930, his style asserted itself, and he achieved some brilliant syntheses. He rediscovered the inspirations of cubism, but interpreted them less severely; his style developed in subtlety, preferring the arabesque to the straight line.

"Braque keeps his distance with regard to pure tones, yet his jade-greens, his sky-blues, his lilacs, his pinks, and his lemon-yellows reveal his sensuous researches into thick and thin paint, sometimes opaque, sometimes translucent, applied in little dabs, punctuated with dotted lines, mixed with plaster and sand, but always plastic, with a feeling of rightness which makes Braque an unrivalled virtuoso."

Then came the magic of his sad, autumnal tones: his ochres, his blacks—so important to him, like the blacks of royal funerals, a whole range of artificial blacks, blacker than black—violets and chestnut-reds, played off against flesh tints and greys heavy as Normandy skies or light as smoke; then, suddenly, a tenderness appeared, bringing with it powder blues and Marie Laurencin pinks, very soon counterbalanced by harder works.

Here, in essence, is what Rebecca West said—rightly—about his colours:

"Braque ranged from the earth to the sky. He took his colours from the earth below him. The basic tones of his early canvases were furnished him by the browns of the soil, the green of grass, and the grey of stone. In the course of the years, he built up a very subtle palette. He was fond of the dull green of greengages, the red verging on black of blackberries, the pale pink of saxifrage blooming on the slopes of the Alps, and other delightful tones. But though he had at one time used a good deal of blue, he had never opened the floodgates and let the colour pour out. Now he used it prodigally, as though his eyes had quit the earth to gaze up at the sky; as though, after spending his life looking at objects in space, he were now focusing his attention on space itself, which constructed objects by defining and illuminating them."

Those places which haunted the painter also give some indication of his colours. There are not many of them: Honfleur, Le Havre, Quimperlé, and Antwerp in the Fauve period of his early career. L'Estaque and La Ciotat, where he played with colours, like a Northerner discovering the sun; then La Roche-Guyon, and then the Midi again; but this time he observed that, as Cézanne had told him, the Midi is colourless in summer. And then Sorgues and Céret with Picasso, where the colour is "internal"; then Paris, where the colour is also "internal"; and in about 1929, he bought some land at Varengeville and had a house built not far from the sea. Maybe it was nostalgia for the light and for the countryside of his childhood, that transparent, heavy light, and the massive coastline of that part of Normandy that attracted him. There he discovered the horizon and the sky.

The Themes in His Work

Let us take an inventory of Braque's paintings. What has he painted? At the very beginning, when he had been vaguely influenced by the impressionists, there were a few realistic portraits: his grandmother and a young girl cousin (p. 20); but on the whole the few human figures which Braque painted during his lifetime were simply human objects treated like

15

mandolins or guitars, with the exception of one nude from the back (p. 19). Apollinaire made this very significant remark: "No one is less concerned with psychology than Braque, and I think he is more affected by a stone than by a face."

Then came a few landscapes painted at Antwerp; for instance, the port, and boats swimming about, as in Marquet's seascapes. Then, at the height of his Fauve period, at L'Estaque: more landscapes, harbours, the countryside, the movements of trees, and quays, which changed into other landscapes, constructed as if from a child's bricks, in which the angles of roofs and the framework of houses could still be identified. But all that passed, and for several years there were only synthetic still lifes, male or female musicians, where all you could see was the scroll of a violin, or the end of a nail or a mandolin. Then further still lifes, more identifiable, containing bottles, pipes, packs of cards, and tables with fruit—plums, lemons, apples, pears (p. 29), and a slice of watermelon, sometimes

16

metamorphosed into a sickle. Sometimes you find Bach or Mozart's name, as if printed on paper, and flowers: sunflowers, bouquets of dahlias, and quantities of green plants. Also, there were fireplaces and overloaded tables (p. 27). This was the intimate side of Braque, which recalls Vuillard through its intimate atmosphere, through its brushwork too, almost *pointilliste* in some places, and through its slightly sad colours, like those in old-fashioned middle-class interiors; even the lamp was a kind of paraffin lamp which does not illuminate anything, because the light comes from elsewhere.

In 1931-32, after he bought his house by the sea, we have still more marine scenes: boats (p. 30) aground beside high cliffs, all fluted and pink, like stucco or artificial marble. Then, at the same time, came large bathing-women (p. 32), also by the seaside, apparently—extremely deformed bathing-women, with small heads, more like the bathers Miró sketched for the ballet *Jeux d'Enfants* than Picasso's giant bathers made at Dinard during the same period. These bathers also at times became still lifes (p. 31): they were evidently constructed in the same way, and for a while the arabesque of the drawing, as if engraved on the canvas, was as important as the colour.

The year 1936 was that of the double-faced women (pp. 35, 53, 54), the period which reminds us most forcibly that we are in the age of speed—airplanes and cars have made huge strides—but this theme, or talent, of double vision (as when you pass rapidly in a car, you see a face and profile almost simultaneously, two heads linked by the same mouth) had already been exploited in the objects and landscapes of the cubists, where we seem to see things simultaneously from the side and from the front, and then both from above and from below.

And then there were hieratic women, like the "Woman with Hat" (p. 35), in stiff, eternal poses, like some of the women in the blood-coloured tapestries of the "Lady and Unicorn," and

17

like some Egyptian frescos in the tombs of the pharaohs, the busts slightly in profile.

And then came more still lifes, but more naturalistic ones. Braque introduced household objects, and the stove of the atelier.

Braque's women—for example, the basket bearers of his earlier period—have scarcely feminine bodies; they have, like Picasso's women, the muscular bodies of athletes with breasts added.

In 1939-40 came the war and—for Braque—sculpture. To tell the truth, it is often a two-dimensional, painter's sculpture.

During the last war, according to Stanislas Fumet, Braque ran short of paints, so he became a sculptor. To give body to his sculptures, he mixed together iron, sand, and even clinkers; later he found in bones and pebbles the materials for the forms which he had to express.

Among these were various subjects which he had never used in his paintings: the most striking thing about them was that they were nearly always in profile.

He had already made a statuette in 1920, a nude which Laurens would have liked—at a distance. He abandoned sculpture, to return to it later. This procedure is characteristic of Braque: he says of his works that they have their origin in a drawn object, take shape very quickly, but then grow slowly, like children; he helps them along, surrounds them with care, until they are able, finally, to live on their own; but I do not believe that Braque likes to leave them, and that is why certain works, conceived much earlier and very beautiful, are taken up again and reworked several years later in the studio.

What were, in fact, the themes of his sculptures? The ibis, triangular fishes, either geometrical (p. 40), or merely round ones, like the dolphin of the Tabernacle d'Assy, ponies, a large head of a horse (p. 45), as beautiful as a head on the Acropolis; and there were also some remarkable female profiles (p. 41)

18

(Continued on page 73)

19

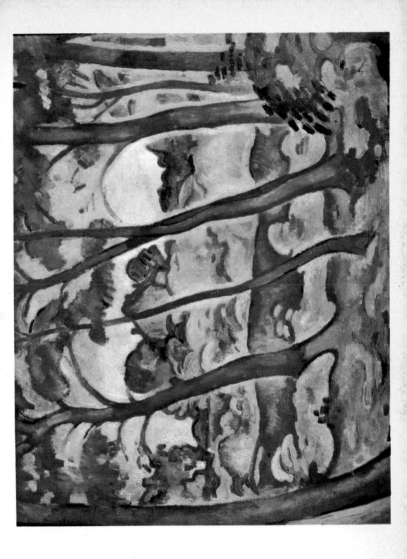

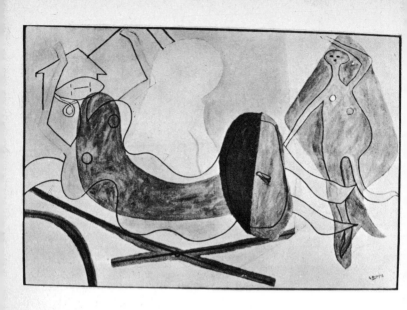

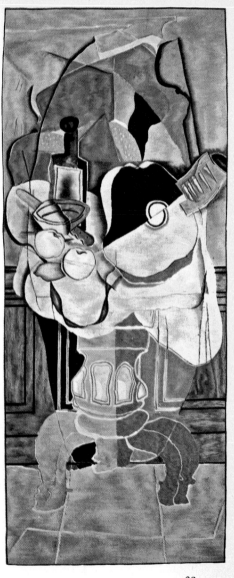

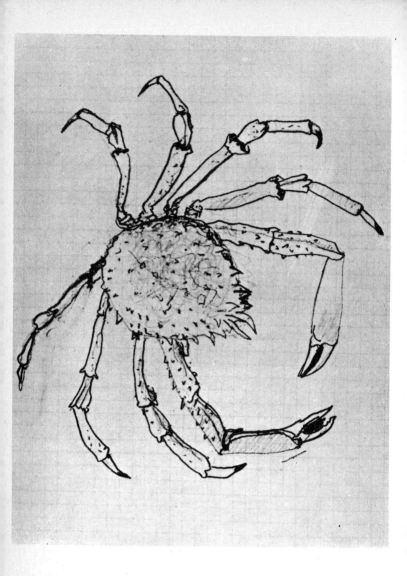

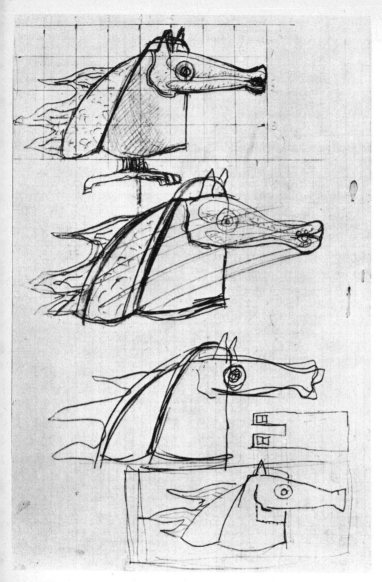

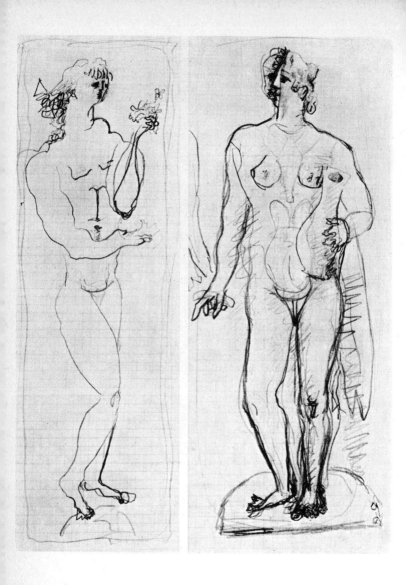

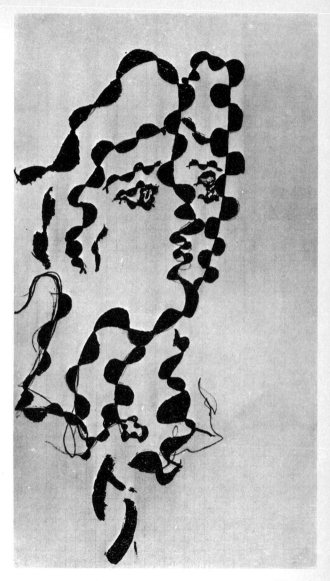

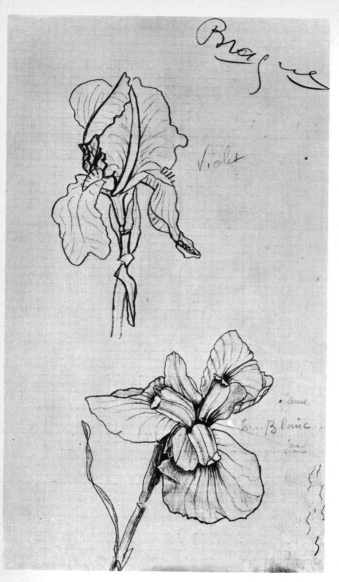

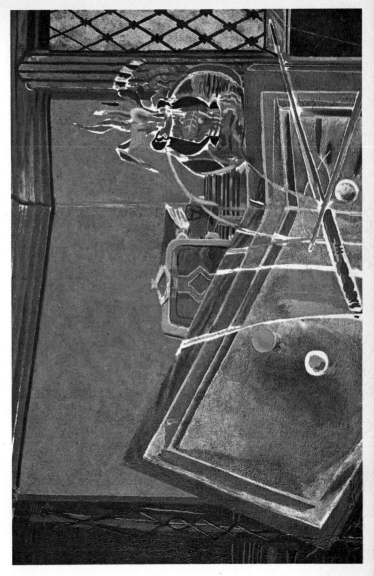

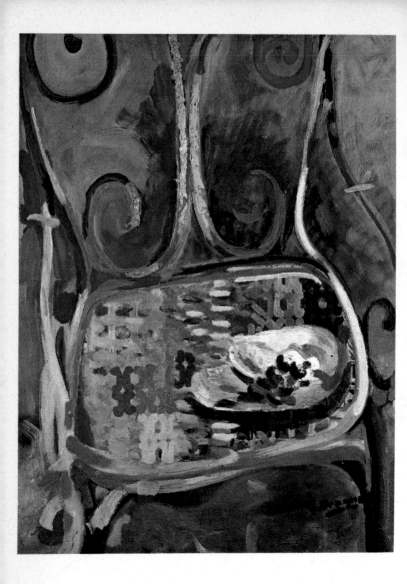

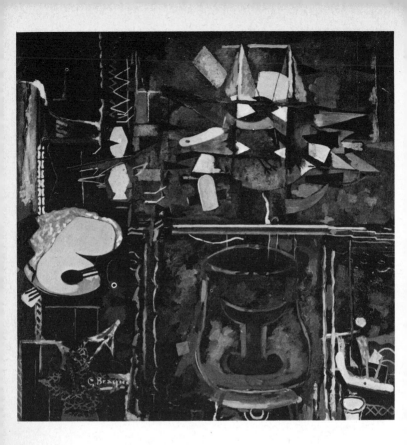

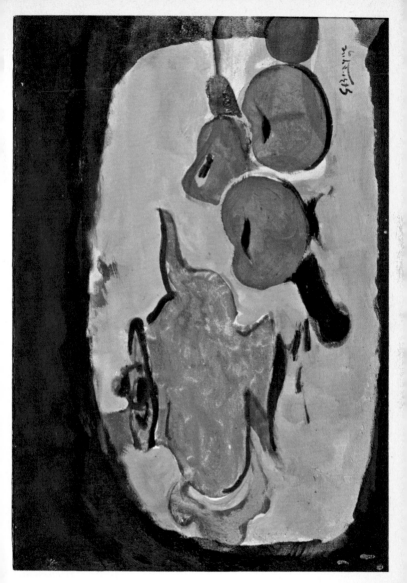

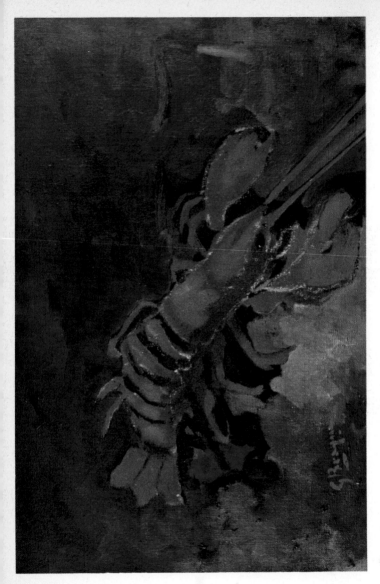

made from soft chalk stones that he gathered on the beaches of Varengeville. But the most beautiful, the most magically primitive, was the "Hymen" (p. 39), constructed like a megalithic monument, with pebbles laid on top of each other, finishing with two heads facing each other and wearing the same hat: a single stone. Braque was the first to construct sculptures with bones, and in this way produced some astonishing bas-reliefs made from the scapulae of sheep.

Finally, in 1932, he invented a process which he used wonderfully: plaster plaques covered with black paint or ink, on which he scratched or hollowed out the design, so that it appeared white, flashing against the black background (p. 38).

These large black-and-white engravings have almost exclusively classical themes: Gieure explains this obsession by Braque's long visits to the Louvre at the beginning of his career—but the painter says that he did not learn any lessons or archetypes of form there, only themes, later to become Helios, Io, Hercules, and therefore myths—which contradicts the [Gieure] story, because they symbolize ideas which Braque takes up again and again almost to the point of obsession.

To sum up, then: they are the sculptures of a painter, spiritual signals made to us by things by virtue of being material creatues and objects: creatures like the fish he made and which, as he looked at them one day, he defined thus: "I have sculptured water."

But I am not going to try to present a complete panorama of Braque's work here, merely to recall the artist's principal themes and periods. It is striking, however, to note how many times the word "cubism" recurs in this study.

This is because cubism has branched out in a number of directions—landscapes, for instance—and has helped Braque to resolve and unify the delicate questions of atmosphere and unity of light. It is the persistence of cubism which has maintained Braque's painting on the highest artistic level, where objects behave in the same way as figures, both being of the same plastic order where painting is concerned; it is also the spirit of cubism which has enabled him to achieve the bone structure of his paintings by ordering their various components and linking them powerfully.

With experience, he felt that he owed it to himself to reassemble the world he had taken to pieces. The component parts of his objects merged more and their relationships became deeper and more intimate.

Braque's art is rich in that indecipherable and magic quality which stamps a great work, and which cubism introduced into art, besides the capacity to suggest the indefinite through the definite, without being caught in the trap of the particular. Braque said: "There is only one thing in art that is worth while: that which cannot be explained."

Birds have often appeared in his paintings since 1948. On this point, Braque says: "One summer, a few years ago, I was in the Camargue. I saw some huge birds flying above the waters. From that vision I derived aerial forms. Birds have inspired me, and I try to make the best use of them that I can in my paintings. While they interest me as living animal species, I have to bury in my memory their natural functions as birds. This concept, even after the shock of inspiration which has brought them to life in my mind, must fade, must be deleted, so that I can draw closer to my essential preoccupation: the construction of pictorial fact. Only painting must impose its presence on what touches it, and metamorphose it afresh; everything that goes to make up the picture must be integrated with this presence, and must efface itself before it."

Braque's birds are of various species: white or black against a royal-blue background, as on the ceiling of the Etruscan Room in the Louvre (p. 63). At times they look like giant seagulls in a

shadow theatre; sometimes, on the contrary, they are very complicated and look as if they have wooden feathers sticking out on all sides, resembling the hulls of boats under construction; sometimes they are as sad and sombre as birds of death, gorged vultures or crows; sometimes they become timid; sometimes, worked into the "Atelier" series (pp. 62, 64), they make a curious spectacle: Braque introduces them, as in his cubist period, like elements dissociated from space and their normal setting, like his printed letters or his pieces of wallpaper. It is odd to note that at certain periods Braque and Picasso have often had analogous ideas. As cubists, they painted the same kind of pictures; ten or twelve years later, they were neo-classicists, and liked to portray gigantic women. But this is not all: Picasso took up the bird motif (in his case, a dove) at the same time as Braque, and Braque's "Ateliers" were followed a few years later by Picasso's Cannes "Ateliers."

Braque's "Ateliers" (pp. 62,64) are a kind of mirage in which the artist evoked his own atelier, a row of canvases against a

75

neutral background, piles of easels, tables heaped with sketch-books, pots of paints and palettes, and various fruit bowls. Sculptures and newspapers may also appear, because all these objects are to be found in the Master's atelier, and they are the subjects of these pictures. The objects are not always painted in a perfectly identifiable form, because Braque is never concerned with presenting things with the slightest degree of realism.

His aim, in the "Ateliers," was, in fact, to pay tribute to the act of painting itself. In other words, "the subject is the picture." These pictures are a microcosm reproducing the painter's professional universe. This phenomenon is due largely to Braque's conviction that "everything changes and relationships vary according to circumstances."

It cannot be said that any object had a unique and constant identity, or even, according to the painter, an existence of its own. This belief has contributed heavily to freeing the artist from his traditional slavery to the objectivity of appearances, and has opened up for him infinite possibilities. It is because of this that Braque was able, in his "Ateliers," to take liberties and to make discoveries which no one before him had ever dreamed of.

He was able to create a kind of fluid, spatial components, into which are dissolved the various objects in the *atelier,* which he afterwards reconstituted in a synthesis of his own invention. It has often been said of Braque that he is the Chardin of the twentieth century. It is true that Chardin had, like Braque, a taste for still lifes, a taste and a feeling for silence, for women changed into statues, for thick, attractive paint, with rich but modest colours. But Chardin's objects—jugs, fish, women, children—although enclosed within their world, meet us halfway, enter our vision, attach themselves to our minds and thoughts by mysterious threads often connected with material reality. With Braque, it is the opposite; there is no substance or reality, but a quality, or lack of image, more or less convincing, which he makes of one object in relation to another. "I ended up," he said, "with a kind of alienation from the object, so as to give it a pictorial meaning, sufficient to its new life. When I paint a vase, it is not to manufacture a utensil capable of holding water, but for another reason. *Objects are recreated to another end:* here, that of taking part in a painting. By losing their normal functions, objects become more human. They are united, therefore, by the relationships which grow up between them and, especially, between them and the painting and myself."

Now let us turn to the *"Carnets intimes"* (pp. 47-53): Braque has been keeping his sketchbooks for some time—possibly fifty years—sketches of what he has made, or what he has wanted to make.

By comparison, every book of Picasso's drawings is revealing, incriminating, proud, imperious, and definitive; at every step, Picasso reveals something of his private life, his encounters with love, dreams, and life. In Braque's drawings, there is not a trace of his private life; each drawing is, I would say, almost timid, shut up in itself, unacknowledged, and very difficult to analyze; he effaces himself. Flowers are flowers, hats are hats, heads of horses are heads of horses, bicycles are bicycles (pp. 46, 47), and there is a great feeling of immobility about them all. He does not play on words, and make puns, but plays with forms: everything is calm, reflective, monastic. Drawings —sketches—ghosts ... Drawings in the style of Dürer, like the lily on page 58.

The artist has, as proved by these sketchbooks, a simplicity which flows from an analysis of complexity pursued for a very long while by a complex mind. Sometimes it is almost like a laboratory analysis, where the scientist, like a surgeon, sees nature and objects unemotionally and with detachment,

Braque's Studio

dealing with them as if they were an engine which a mechanic
has to analyze, even repair.

Braque, the silent man, the solitary man as Léger called him, is
an immense and secretive painter. "I perceive," Léger reiterat-
ed, "that this work is immense, a fine example of fidelity to
painting." He points out that there is an astonishing unity
throughout Braque's deepening of a few initial themes, striking
because of the apparent monotony of his inspiration, "themes
which are repeated, but which are slowly metamorphosed in a
perpetual search for methods, the research into space, and its
conquest."

Ideas fade away to the extent that the painting advances.

Braque says: "I know exactly where I am going. My goal is
my desire to make paintings of the utmost significance."

His work has no breaks, no seismic shocks, like Picasso's.
Braque is the painter who succeeded in placing a dirty *bidet* or a
dubious washbasin in the finest gilded salons of millionaires

because, for him, "the best part of art consists of discovering what is 'common'."

What could be more ordinary than a lemon, than a still life with an apple and a pipe; boring, in theory, and yet this lemon and this pipe are worth thousands of pounds—because they are the guardians of a mystery.

The Anguish of Man and the Mystery of Creation

The more you progress in the Master's work (and by "progress" I mean know, study, and live with his pictures or reproductions of them), the more you sense a kind of anguish, like that which emanates from Goya. I do not make this comparison lightly. It is perhaps his only point of contact with Goya, apart from his colours, his use of blacks, greys, and pinks, and a certain apparent confusion in the delimitation of forms.

I am aware of drama when I look at these women with two faces, at "The Night" (p. 61), or at the birds which have become heavy flying machines. The atmosphere of the "Ateliers" is oppressive, and it is very painful in the other interiors; you could not live in it. This anguish is strongly present, even in the still lifes, and is a world to itself. Each picture is a sitting *in camera*.

To return to his birds: bird-planes, heavy and powerful, like some kind of air transport for a hundred people, sinister as vultures, like danger signals. When he paints a bird and its nest (p. 65), in every case it is no longer a real bird; it is more of an arabesque, the ghost of a bird. And the nest has lost its function as a nest, lost in the imagined anecdote of representation, but it has recovered its mystery—mystery of the world's creation, of the total space of the picture.

With Braque—and this is why I refer to metamorphoses—this striking fact must especially be noted: everything becomes

79

"other" than what it is, it has another dimension, another *raison d'être*.

"To construct," says Braque, "is to assemble homogeneous elements. The Palace of Versailles, or a letter by Madame de Sévigné developed in this way."

Solid painting and play with metamorphoses: two terms which are, in fact, contradictory, yet correctly explain his work.

The life which springs from his canvases is sometimes tumultuous, but always interior. In all his canvases there are waves of something profound, but of something profoundly mobile beneath the apparent immobility. He has often tried to create this sense of movement, but it is a movement frozen between the Egyptian and the Assyrian: like a bird in flight, but which, at the same time, hovers; yet you are aware that its heart is beating.

And you can sense, too, in his works, a kind of massive ground-swell, capable of moving anything. Also, *"Braque le Patron"* has a pugnacious, Icelandic fisherman side to him, capable, I feel sure, of terrible inner rages.

His work is immense and calls for deep thought.

Sometimes the material plays its pure game, disturbing as a disease of the skin. Some pictures are very strongly painted, yet light; others are attacked with a thick knife; still others are done entirely by means of light—I am thinking of his "Plains," those pictures of wheatfields painted in 1950, which are like his pictures of sad sunflowers (p. 70), or that enormous black bird (p. 69), like a sort of homage to the tortured Van Gogh.

Braque is a magician: only he can open a window (p. 57) the way he does, balance an apple so unsteadily, make so lopsided a pedestal table stand upright, that the objects live or exist on such different planes of perspective.

You can imagine yourself at home, rearranging, for your own amusement, a still life by Chardin, by Zurbarán, or even by Juan Gris; but it would be impossible to rearrange a still life by Braque, because it really only exists on canvas, and that is the miracle. It is untranslatable, inimitable.

Braque, with his baroque fantasy, his acute concept of painting, knows that painting is mysterious reference and a thing of the mind. He is a painter who is both human and inhuman because, if he paints simple things, it is so as to deceive you the more, to mislead you; and that is his aim. Art, he says, is meant to disturb you; science, to reassure you.

And those jagged shapes, slashed out of those strange cloths on his pedestal tables, always look as if they are supported by the ectoplasm of some medium, their master.

Art and life interweave. Braque says:

"With cubism, Picasso and I have transformed the face of the war; before us, there was impressionism and blue horizons; after us, whole armies have been camouflaged as cubists. First of all, there are colours and forms. Much has been said about the cubist object. The important thing is that these colours and these forms interact, animate one another. The problem is that of grey and white on the canvas becoming a pitcher and a

napkin. The colours are conceived even before it is known what they will be. I have written: *Things do not exist, only relationships exist.* I am often asked: 'What is the name of that bird, of that flower?' I reply: 'I do not know. Ask the experts who know the names of things. I want an object to lose its normal purpose; it is only then that art confers its universal character on it. When what is, at first, a white mark becomes a cloth, the plastic has become the poetic'."

And here are some more of the Master's words:

"We shall never rest; the present is everlasting."

"It is the precariousness of the work which gives the artist his heroic stance."

"Action is a series of desperate acts which permit you to keep on hoping."

"Emotion neither adds, nor copies itself; it is the seed, the work is the flowering."

According to Jean Paulhan, someone looking at a still life once said to him: "But that light isn't in nature."

"So I'm not in nature, then?"

"But where does that light come from?"

"Oh, that's from another canvas you don't know."

"Some read fortunes from tea leaves," says Braque; "I read from pigment."

We end on this sorcerer's explanation:

"When I begin, it is as if my picture were on the other side, merely covered with that white dust—the canvas. All I have to do is wipe off the dust. I have a little broom to free the blue, another for the green or the yellow: my paint brushes. When everything has been cleaned, the picture is finished."

LIST OF ILLUSTRATIONS